ALWAYS PLENTY OF LIGHT AT THE STARLIGHT ALL NIGHT DINER

Darcy Parker Bruce

BROADWAY PLAY PUBLISHING INC
New York
www.broadwayplaypublishing.com
info@broadwayplaypublishing.com

First edition: November 2020
I S B N: 978-0-88145-885-5

Book design: Marie Donovan
Page make-up: Adobe InDesign
Typeface: Palatino

ALWAYS PLENTY OF LIGHT AT THE STARLIGHT ALL NIGHT DINER was first produced at Know Theatre of Cincinnati (Andrew Hungerford, Producing Artistic Director; Tamara Winters Associate Artistic Director) opening on 22 February 2019 and closing on 16 March. The cast and creative contributors were:

SAM ....Lormarev Jones
JESSA .... Leah Strasser
DR MOXIE...Michael Burnham
DANNI..Maggie Cramer

Director.. Alice Flanders

Scenic & Lighting Designer ....Andrew Hungerford
Costume Designer......................... Noelle Wedig-Johnston
Sound & Projections Designer ....Douglas Borntrager
Stage Manager ....Meghan Winter
Props Master.. Becca Armstrong

CHARACTERS

SAM, *(late 30s, NB) overnight janitor at the Starlight. Very observant, hard on the outside but a real softie on the inside. Totally and hopelessly in love with* JESSA *(see below). Lives in her truck. Sometimes couch-surfs or catches a break with a generous lady. Loves the Starlight second only to* JESSA, *but that's debatable. Prone to motion sickness induced by sudden Time Travel™.*

JESSA, *(early to mid 30s, F) late-shift waitress at the Starlight. Very pregnant. Subsists on coconut cream pie, due to baby-sickness and the fact that she can't keep anything else down. Very confused about her dopey husband, Johnny.*

DR. FRANKLIN MOXIE PHD, *(older than time, M) doctor! Time travel enthusiast! Eccentric weirdo! Adorable savant! Coffee guzzler and frequent patron of the Starlight, he is a SCIENTIST who knows way more than you do about SCIENCE. Also, time, space, continuums, etc. Absolutely dashing in a white lab coat. A glutton for pie.*

DANNI, *(early 20s, NB)* DR. MOXIE's *graduate assistant (read: slave), baseball fan and TOTAL dino buff, she knows more about the Cretaceous and the Diamondbacks than most folks in Arizona. Loves to read. Collects baseball cards and is also just the right amount of concerned about that comet—you know the one—that's supposed to pass by Earth tonight? That big streak of white light in the night sky?*

NEWS REPORTER, *cany gender, enthusiastic to a fault*

SETTING

The Starlight All Night Diner, Arizona. Somewhere in the desert, where the sky stretches vast overhead, the days are long and hot, and the nights are cold and lonely.

Time: Now. Also the EXTREME past. Like. Dinosaurs. Because Time Travel.™

NOTES

Dialogue with a dash at the end represents rapid interruption. A slash within a line indicates overlapping speech. Lack of punctuation is intentional, and an indicator that the words be read in a rush, or as a run on sentence. Lack of capital letters may indicate a character isn't feeling very confident.

This is a fast play with pockets of silence.

In any given production there should be a strong diversity of casting. Any character may be played by any queer identified person, and Danni and Sam's pronouns should change as needed with that casting. This is NOT just a play about white/cis lesbian identity, it's a celebration of intersectional queerness and should be cast as such.

NOTE ON MUSIC

For performance of copyrighted songs, arrangements
or recordings referenced in this play, permission
of the copyright owner(s) must be obtained. Other
songs, arrangements or recordings may be substituted
provided permission from the copyright owner(s) of
such songs, arrangements or recordings is obtained
or songs, arrangements or recordings in the public
domain may be substituted.

(Lights up on a small diner, the Starlight. It's about as small as the Milky Way when you're gazing at it from the hood of a '98 Chevrolet. It's cozy but glamorous. The counters are a deep dark blue, just like those pockets of outer space you can almost see into, and the floor is a replica of the moon's surface based on photos from the 1969 moon landing. The ceiling is made out of glass that looks like stars which hang all around so that it doesn't seem like there's a ceiling at all, really.)

(On the counter there is an old radio broadcasting a set of the oldies. There is also a large coffee pot with several burners keeping coffee warm.)

(Close by is a rickety wooden ladder, and balanced upon it is SAM, *nursing a cup of coffee and polishing the stars.* SAM *is wearing dirty jeans, and a coffee stained shirt. She has several filthy rags hanging out of her back pocket. She's humming along to the radio.)*

*(*JESSA *is behind the counter, leaning and watching* SAM *as she cleans.* JESSA *wears an apron, which does little to conceal her very pregnant state.)*

JESSA: He's depressed.

SAM: Depressed.

JESSA: Depressed. He's eating tons of—of junk. I don't buy it for him. Frozen pizzas, fast food, you know. And he isn't sleeping.

SAM: *I* don't sleep—

JESSA: *You* don't count—

SAM: —I'd *like* to sleep—

JESSA: —try a *real* bed, and not just the back of your Chevy—

SAM: —don't insult my truck—

JESSA: —it's *hardly* a truck—

SAM: —and I've got a date later—

JESSA: —at what like three A M? It's almost midnight—

SAM: —she works late. And yes, three A M and *she's* got a bed so—

JESSA: —you need your *own* bed—

SAM: —it's on my list—

JESSA: —so I've heard—

SAM: —but we were talking about Johnny, not me—

JESSA: —You're as bad as he is. You've cleaned that star like four times Sam—

SAM: —just want to make sure *(She polishes it one more time.)* see the way the light hits it?

JESSA: Gorgeous. You're good at your job.

SAM: I know.

JESSA: *(Beat)* He won't stop watching television.

SAM: —well that's normal. Does he scratch himself?

JESSA: Don't be such a man-hater. *(Beat)* Yes. Yes he does. *(Beat)* We're having a baby! We're having a baby, like, any second, and he doesn't even seem excited. I'm telling you, Sam, he's depressed. He's always been quiet but this is different, this is, this is underground. You know?

SAM: *(Teasing)* Like a dinosaur?

JESSA: Like, waaaaaay underground because it's like, he's got all this dirt over his head, he's asleep, or tucked away and he can't hear me or baby Mae *(She touches her stomach.)* and I, well I just feel like I'm floating. Like a bird or a balloon and if it weren't for him I'd just float away—

SAM: *(Drinking coffee)* Okay but then where would you go, huh?

JESSA: —lately I've been wondering what it might be like to, just, I don't know, just drift.

SAM: So *(Beat)* drift.

JESSA: It's not that easy. I'm not like *you*—

SAM: Then—

JESSA: Then. Then. I bring him frozen dinners and we sit on the couch together and when he gets too quiet I put his hand on my stomach and I listen, you know. To Mae. And I hope he listens too.

SAM: *(She has been cleaning the stars, but pauses to look down at JESSA.)* It's late.

JESSA: It's late.

SAM: You hungry?

JESSA: No, no it's fine—

SAM: You've got to eat kid. *(She climbs off the ladder, wipes her hands on a rag.)* Come on. Sit down.

(Upon seeing JESSA's hesitation:)

SAM: There's no one here. You're not going to get in trouble.

JESSA: Oh. Oh fine. My feet are killing me, Sam, my dogs are barking, can you hear them? Woof woof! so loud! *(She laughs.)* I can't wait for this kid to break free of me!

(JESSA sits with SAM's help.)

JESSA: oof. you won't tell?

SAM: Do I ever? *(Beat)* So what's on the menu, let's see—coconut crème pie?

JESSA: Baby Mae's favorite!

SAM: *(Walking to grab her a slice of pie from a fridge behind the counter)* At least it's not pickles and ice cream.

JESSA: I'm so glad you don't mind me talking to you about all this. You know, about Johnny and the baby and, and just—

SAM: Floating? Flying? *(She brings the pie over)* Running away?

JESSA: Oh I'm not going anywhere you know? If I haven't left yet—

SAM: It's not so bad here it's really—I mean, the Starlight *(She makes a grand gesture)* is there anywhere else even half as beautiful?

JESSA: Outer space?

SAM: *(Smiles)* Yeah, Jessa, yeah. Outer space.

(There is a moment of silence, the radio plays softly in the background. JESSA eats and SAM returns to the ladder, folding it up and tucking it into a corner.)

JESSA: Ow! Ooh, ow, oh!

SAM: What's wrong is it the baby are you okay?

JESSA: Oh no it's my feet, it's my feet these shoes are *killing* me.

SAM: You want some help?

JESSA: *(Looks sheepish)* Yes. Please—

(SAM approaches JESSA as though she has done this a hundred times before, and tenderly kneels in front of her, removing her shoes. All the while JESSA looks down at her, the moment is sweet, comforting, and—if you will— pregnant. SAM takes her time. This goes on in silence until the second shoe is almost off)

SAM: You know. You know—I—

JESSA: *(She wiggles her toes.)* That feels good that feels so nice, it's much better— *(A sigh of relief)* Yeah?

SAM: I just wonder, I mean, Johnny's away so much, and when he's home, I mean—

JESSA: *(As if she knows what SAM is struggling to say)* Uh-huh?

SAM: Are you happy, Jessa? Are you, I mean with Johnny? and of course you're happy what's wrong with me what am I thinking, of course, you've got, you've got a baby on the way and a husband who adores you and—

(The door to the diner flies open. Enter DR MOXIE trailing a stream of loose papers, followed immediately by DANNI, who struggles in vain to catch the paper trail.)

(DR MOXIE is older, stately, and dashing in his white lab coat. DANNI is skinny, wearing a plain white t, cuffed jeans, and a baseball cap. Think The Great Gilly Hopkins but all grown up. She looks a little frantic.)

DR MOXIE: TURN ON THE NEWS! COFFEE! WE NEED COFFEE!

(SAM and JESSA are momentarily stunned, their quiet moment blown from the water as if it were a turtle and DR MOXIE a particularly well aimed shot gun.)

(DR MOXIE and DANNI make their way to the counter, where the good doctor sits leaving his assistant to fiddle with the radio.)

(Static, and then a news report. During the report SAM and JESSA collect themselves, and SAM begins to clean tables while JESSA pours coffee.)

NEWS REPORTER: —have your eyes locked on the skies folks! Less than forty minutes to go, have you shut your lights off yet? Cities all over our great state of

Arizona have been powering down in the last hour, so make sure to give yourselves at least twenty minutes of true darkness in order to let your eyes adjust. Look up! Look up good people to the stars above and if you see that faint green glow then raise a mighty cry and call your family to the grand outdoors, pull them away from all their vices and devices and demand that they attend to this celestial event—

(The voice cuts off as DANNI *turns off the radio)*

DANNI: Damn boss—they got it all wrong—

DR MOXIE: Still *excited*! Still *thrilled*! Little do they know

*(*JESSA *hands* DR MOXIE *his coffee.)*

DR MOXIE: thank you my dear—little do they know!

SAM: Late night, Doctor?

DR MOXIE: Isn't it always? Who can sleep? SCIENCE!

DANNI: *(She nods at* SAM *and* JESSA*)* Hey Sam, Jessa. How's baby Mae?

JESSA: Kicking the shit out of me, currently, but otherwise fine and dandy—

DANNI: Lost your shoes?

JESSA: —don't be a pain.

DANNI: *(She smiles)* Can I get some coffee? It's going to be a long night. *(*JESSA *hands her a coffee)*

SAM: Seems like it already is—

DR MOXIE: *(Demanding)* The two of you! Are you the only ones here?

JESSA: Aren't we always?

DR MOXIE: Good. Good. *(He gathers his papers close and examines them.)* Danni!

DANNI: Yeah boss—

DR MOXIE: Calculations?

(DANNI *goes through the papers until she turns up the right ones.* DR MOXIE *seems satisfied, and is lost in his work.)*

DANNI: You, uh, you need me to work anything out or?

DR MOXIE: *(Waving her away)* Sh!

(DANNI *returns to her stool. She removes some baseball cards from her back pocket and begins to shuffle them.* SAM *comes up behind her and tweaks her hat.)*

SAM: Danni. How's it goin?

DANNI: *(Clearly flustered)* oh you know it's going great pretty good that is I mean, Dr Moxie's got it all planned out you know so there's that but I'm not so sure—

SAM: What is happening with the two of you?

JESSA: And where have you been? We haven't seen you in almost a week!

DANNI: Oh, *(Forced laughter)* oh! Well! Well, uh well you see, there's um. Okay *(Composing herself, though still clearly nervous around* SAM. *She cracks her knuckles, takes a deep breath.)* okay. Well, see, what's happening is that the good doctor thinks, and so do I, actually, *we* think, that um that earth might be in for a bit of a uh well, a *celestial event.*

JESSA: Well yeah, we know that. We heard it on the radio along with everybody else.

DANNI: *(Forced laughter again)* yeah. Yeah! Uh. The comet. Comet Killjoy, an ironic name, actually because it probably will, uh kill all the joy there is. On earth. Also life as we know it.

(DANNI *takes a sip of her coffee.* SAM *and* JESSA *stare at her.)*

JESSA: What?

SAM: Yeah, what are you talking about Danni?

DANNI: *(She paws through her baseball cards as if searching for comfort.)* Well, thing is, we're in for um, less of a *celestial event* and more of a, well, an *impact event. (Beat)* it's not a comet. It's an asteroid. And it's going to hit us.

(There is a moment of silence, JESSA *looks baffled, and* SAM *lets out a heavy sigh.)*

SAM: Danni. Danni. Listen, I know you love Dr Moxie, and I think he's brilliant, I do, I really do. But don't you think that maybe just a little bit there's a chance he might be *(Another sigh)* overreacting?

DANNI: Um. *(She is conflicted. She doesn't want to contradict* SAM*)* um. No.

SAM: Okay Danni. You go to University of Arizona right?

DANNI: Uh huh.

SAM: And what is it you study, I can never remember.

DANNI: *(With pride, totally puffed up)* Getting my Masters in Atmospheric Sciences with a minor in Astro-bio.

SAM: Right. Right. Great. You're kind of a whiz right? Kid genius?

DANNI: *(Still totally puffed)* Youngest in my program.

SAM: Okay. So maybe, there at U of A, and you with all of your infinite knowledge of space and physics etc. etc. Maybe, you can understand how Dr Moxie, *might* be mistaken?

DANNI: *(Completely scandalized)* He's the *chair* of the *department!*

SAM: *(Sighs)* Okay kid.

DANNI: I'm twenty four—

SAM: Okay *(Searching)* Danni okay. When are we due this, impact?

DANNI: What time is it now?

JESSA: Eleven thirty three.

DANNI: Um ok, then about uh twenty-six minutes. Give or take.

JESSA: That's crazy. That can't be right—can it, Sam? Can that be right?

SAM: I doubt it. *(Beat)* But I'm no whiz kid.

DANNI: *(Staring at the cards)* You guys shouldn't freak out. Don't worry, the good doctor has a plan. It's just, um, it's just that—

SAM: Let it out.

DANNI: *(Suddenly urgent, moving towards* DR MOXIE*)* Doc, are you *sure* we can't try to take the Diamondbacks with us? I think, I mean, *(She pulls calculations from her pockets and they spill on the floor along with the baseball cards.)* I crunched some numbers and I think we can handle it—

DR MOXIE: *(Not unkindly)* This is no time for *(With disdain)* sports, Danni. No time at all. We've talked about this. It's too risky. We can't chance it.

DANNI: Doc!

DR MOXIE: No. No not at all no and let that be the last of it! Pie!

DANNI: Pi? 3.14 *(Etc)*

DR MOXIE: No, *pie*. With an "e". Coconut. Jessa?

JESSA: Coming right up doc, though you should know, you're depriving me of vital nutrients necessary to the well being of myself and my unborn child— *(Beat)* You look like you could use a laugh doc.

DR MOXIE: I'm saving my laughter for later, Jessa. Sometime after midnight.

SAM: Alright. Alright I need a break from this. I'm going out for a smoke. I'll be sure to 'raise a mighty cry' if I catch sight of our doom.

DANNI: No need. Haven't you been outside at all tonight? It's shining up there, a streak of bright white!

(SAM *takes a minute, looks annoyed, and heads outdoors.*)

JESSA: But the radio—

DR MOXIE: FOOLS!

DANNI: Yeah. The news is being super shifty about this whole thing. They can't wrap their heads around it.

DR MOXIE: You mean they're lying.

JESSA: I don't understand. Why? Should I be worried? Should I get Johnny, should I call my mother? (*Beat*) we have a dog—

(SAM *enters, concerned.*)

SAM: Yeah that's some bright light.

JESSA: Sam! I'm going home, I've got to head home can you call Tommy for me, call and see if Erica can come in instead? It was supposed to be her tonight anyway!

SAM: Well hold on hold on let's see, I don't get it, if it's so obvious, I mean it's right there for everyone to see, shouldn't the whole world be freaking out?

(SAM *moves to the radio, pauses, turns it on, everyone but* DR MOXIE *watches.*)

NEWS REPORTER: —sure is some bright light folks! And just think, it's going to pass right by us in less then one half hour! Grab your blankets and your picnic baskets, your wine and your loved ones, and watch those skies!

(SAM *turns to another station and Elvis can be heard softly*)

JESSA: They're not even a little bit concerned—

DANNI: —try N P R—

DR MOXIE: Just stay put would you? *(He is looking through papers, eating his pie)* don't go anywhere. Sometimes the best thing to do is to take a moment to relish the ordinary.

DANNI: Who's that boss?

DR MOXIE: A Moxie original. You can credit me later.

JESSA: You don't think, I mean, I should go home, shouldn't I?

SAM: Call Johnny. You'll feel better if you do. And you know Tommy's just going to give you shit if you dash.

JESSA: And I'm not in the mood for that tonight.

SAM: No-one's in the mood for that ever.

JESSA: Yeah okay I'll call him. *(She heads behind the counter, pulls out a phone, dials Johnny.)*

DANNI: I'm going to get those jars from the car boss. *(She exits.)*

JESSA: Hi, hi hey Johnny! You're still up good. *(Pause)* What? The dog food? In the bottom cupboard. You haven't fed her yet? *(Pause)* No. No it's fine it's okay. Are you going to sleep soon? *(Pause)* Yeah yeah I know I just thought that maybe. Okay. Well have you been outside? *(Pause)* Yeah outside, it's a nice night. *(Beat)* there's going be a comet! Killjoy. *(Pause)* uh huh. Well yeah I guess it is kind of a funny name. Listen, Johnny, listen you should go outside go take a peek. *(Beat)* I'll wait.

(A long pause, during which DANNI reenters with a case of mason jars and a bag swinging from her shoulder, DANNI sets the jars down at a booth and begins to take them out of the flat and inspect them.)

JESSA: No, no I'm still here. Did you go outside did you see it?*(Pause)* Oh Yeah! Yeah it's really bright you should— *(Pause)* oh, yeah okay no. I love Lucy too. *(Pause)* That's a good episode. *(Pause)* Okay. Love you. Baby Mae too. *(She hangs up the phone.)*

SAM: How's Johnny?

JESSA: He's good. Fine. I made him go outside.

SAM: Do you feel any better?

JESSA: Yeah. I'm good I'm great.

SAM: You're *lying.*

JESSA: I'm *fine.* *(Beat)* it's probably nothing.

SAM: The comet?

DR MOXIE: ASTEROID!

JESSA: The *comet.* It's probably nothing. I feel. I feel a little—

(DANNI spots something. She grabs a jar, sneaks up to it, slams the jar over it.)

DANNI: Got it!

SAM: Got what?

DANNI: A lizard! See? *Urosaurus ornatus. (She examines it.)* An ornate tree lizard. He's a male. See the blue patches?

SAM: *(Disinterested)* Pretty— *(To* JESSA*)* you feel?

JESSA: Just a little. Unsure. *(Beat)* Lonely. I feel, lonely.

SAM: *(She crosses to* JESSA.*)* even with Mae?

JESSA: *(Beat)* oh you're right I'm being silly this is ridiculous—Dr Moxie you went and got me in such a funk!

DR MOXIE: "The obscure we see eventually. The completely obvious, it seems, takes longer."

SAM: Howard Smith?

DR MOXIE: Edward Murrow

SAM: Ah.

DANNI: *(Staring at the lizard)* He wants to get out. He keeps trying to climb the sides, but he can't get a grip on the glass—

DR MOXIE: —are you contaminating our specimen jars Danni? That seems ill advised.

DANNI: *(Admonished)* No. I mean. Sorry. Yeah. I'll let him go. Outside. Or inside?

DR MOXIE: *Outside* Danni.

DANNI: Right yes right. *(She takes urosaurus ornatus outdoors, re-enters.)* It's going to be really different.

DR MOXIE: Either way it will be different. You need only choose which you prefer. Time?

DANNI: *(She checks her watch)* eleven forty two.

DR MOXIE: Jessa! More coffee, please—

JESSA: We're almost out—should I make a new pot—

DR MOXIE: —NOT YET! *(Beat)* I'll drink the dregs. I'll want a new pot in about, seventeen minutes.

JESSA: *(Pouring the dregs)* you are extra cryptic tonight doc. Danni, coffee?

DANNI: Not yet. Thanks.

(The Starlight is quiet once more. DANNI examines her baseball cards. DR MOXIE is still going through papers, drinking his coffee. JESSA measures out the grounds for a new pot, and SAM is still wiping down the countertops. The radio plays something like Presley's All Shook Up.)

SAM: *(Cleaning)* are you worried about the comet?

JESSA: I mean, probably not—are you?

SAM: No. No definitely not. *(Wiping furiously)*

JESSA: *(To* SAM*)* You know those are clean right?

SAM: What?

JESSA: Those counter tops. You've been cleaning them for an hour. You can probably stop now.

SAM: Oh. Oh I just, I—okay. *(Beat, she puts down the rag)*

JESSA: Sam. Are you alright?

SAM: Yeah, yes. *(A sigh)* Are *you* alright?

JESSA: I have this weird feeling. I can't explain it? That sounds silly.

SAM: It's *not* silly. I think I know what you mean—uh—Jessa—jessa look. Maybe I should tell you something—

JESSA: *(Eagerly)* Yeah?

SAM: Um. Um— *(Closer, closer—beat, she can't)* You know the reason I love the Starlight?

JESSA: Is it the grease stains on the walls? Is it the way the stench of fried food permeates your clothes at night? Is it the long hours?

SAM: None of that none of that it's it's how, look at these stars *(She gestures to the ceiling.)* and, and this floor *(Again, gesture)* being here, being in the Starlight it's like being—like being everywhere at once.

JESSA: Okay. *(A small soft smile)* okay I get that.

SAM: *(Encouraged)* It's like being in the center of the universe. And something about that, for me, it's always been really really good because I don't feel so, so out of control, when I'm here. And yeah, it's a diner in the middle of nowhere and sure, Tommy's a dick but these late nights, just you and me and the rhythm of keeping it all going, I mean when I leave, where do I go? My Chevy. And maybe sometimes a different sort of small space, with someone I don't know that well—but here in the Starlight, it's *(Beat)* bigger. *(She pauses. This was a lot for her,)* Um, you know? I, I guess what I'm trying to say is, don't don't feel lonely or scared because when you're here, you—you can see *(She is self conscious, feeling lame.)* everything.

JESSA: You know what I really love about this smelly messy diner in the middle of this nowhere desert?

SAM: What?

JESSA: It doesn't matter that it's in the middle of a nowhere desert. It doesn't matter that it's only as big as the house I grew up in. When I'm here with you—when I'm here—um. In the Starlight—I feel like any second I could be somewhere else. You know? Somewhere different than anywhere I've ever been. It feels like the whole universe is in here and—

SAM: —and—

JESSA: —I love how safe it makes me feel.

(There is another silence, laced with the sounds of the radio, papers rustling, coffee being sipped. Outside, the light from the comet grows brighter and brighter.)

DANNI: *(Very conscious of the moment)* So do you guys like dinosaurs or?

(Once again SAM and JESSA are jolted out of their reverie. They stare at DANNI.)

SAM: *(Annoyed)* Dinosaurs?

DANNI: Yeah, you know, feathery, kind of—giant and uh— *(Her cell phone rings, she pulls it out, sees the caller I D, scowls)* oh, I gotta—I gotta take this. *(She answers.)* hey mom. *(She walks away.)* I'm glad you called me back—

SAM: I *know* what dinosaurs are—

(Spot on DANNI on the phone in the corner.)

DANNI: Mom. Mom, hey listen. I'm glad you got back to me I gotta talk to you—uh, there's some stuff, is dad home? *(Pause)* Yeah? Can you, can you put him on too? *(Pause)* Hey dad. I miss you both yeah. *(Pause)* No everything's fine—okay everything's *not* fine. You guys see that light in the sky? *(Pause)* no see it's not a comet actually it's an ast— *(Pause)* what? What? That's not why I called— *(Pause)* Brit? No, uh no we broke up— *(Pause)* No. That does not mean I've 'come to my senses,' that means she was a gin guzzling nitwit who thought some douchey frat-bro at the bar was worth throwing—you know what never mind, it's not a fun story. For me. *(Pause)* yeah but it's not a 'phase'. *(Growing cold)* uh huh. Uh huh. Uh huh. *(Pause)* Jason sounds like a real chump—champ! I mean champ. Uh huh. No. that's awesome, actually go ahead. Invite him over. *(Pause)* next Friday night? Great. Yeah. Around seven. Meatloaf? Sure. I've been a vegetarian for the last four years, but meatloaf sounds great. *(Pause)* I am *not* using my sarcasm to mask my feel—okay. *(Pause)* The green dress? *(She looks at her watch, looks out the window)* You know what? Yes. I will wear the green dress. I'll uh—shave my legs, and I'll see if Nikki will let me borrow her pumps— *(Pause)* No that's not *slang* for "what I do"— *(Pause)* Mom—listen I—would it really be that bad? If I was, you know if I was um more like, um Jason? You always wanted a—son—right? *(Choked laughter)* Mom? *(Pause)* Hey Dad. *(Pause)* I'm not trying to work her up, but it would be really stellar if you guys could just— *(Pause)* okay. Ok not another word. I'll see you *Friday. (Pause)* Yeah. Yeah. The sky sure is bright. *(Pause)* love you too.*(She hangs up, stands still for a minute, then—)* FUCK.

(Without a beat, DR MOXIE rises and brings DANNI the rest of his pie. He makes her sit. SAM and JESSA come over.)

SAM: That was—rough. You okay?

DR MOXIE: "Discussion is an exchange of knowledge; an argument an exchange of ignorance." Robert Quillen.

JESSA: Danni. Sweety. It's not you. It's them.

DANNI: Thanks guys. I know. It's just—god I can't stand it! and they wonder why I don't come home to visit—

DR MOXIE: Danni. When I hired you, what did I say I was looking for?

DANNI: *(A beat as she tries to remember correctly.)* A comparably high functioning biped capable of some terrestrial motion, regardless of how that might be achieved, adept at solving complex mathematical equations who enjoys one-sided loquacious debates and also pie. *(Beat)* With an "e".

DR MOXIE: That's correct. And did I mention anything about your personal life?

DANNI: I mean that thing about the pie was a little personal—

DR MOXIE: —Danni—did I exhibit any signs of interest in your personal preferences?

DANNI: No doc.

DR MOXIE: You are, I presume, aware of the unique sexual assignment given to the flatworm, the sponge, most species of snails, and all earthworms?

DANNI: Hermaphroditic, sir.

DR MOXIE: And throughout time has this helped their species to flourish, or to—how would you put it—*flop*?

DANNI: Flourish, sir—but I'm not, um…I don't have— uh—

DR MOXIE: —my point, I'm certain, has not been lost— *(It has)*

JESSA: He's right, Danni—and don't forget about seahorses and penguins and—

SAM: Hey, I read that book—

DR MOXIE: *(Perking up) Biological Exuberance?*

SAM: *—And, uh, Tango Makes Three.*

DR MOXIE: *(A little disgusted)* Ah.

DANNI: *(With a sigh)* Thanks guys. This was the, the *weirdest* pep talk ever.

JESSA: We'll be your family Danni. If you don't mind having us.

SAM: You know you can always talk to me, about— whatever.

DANNI: I know thanks. *(Beat)* It's just, I— *(She takes out her baseball cards)* I *called* to try and, and get them to—

(DR MOXIE clears his throat,)

(They all look to DR MOXIE expectantly.)

DR MOXIE: We don't have much time.

SAM: Wow Doc could you *be* more macabre.

JESSA: *(Grabbing SAM's arm)* Um. God. I've got goosebumps.

SAM: *(Flustered by JESSA's closeness)*You do? *(She looks.)* You do! What, what from all of this—from the comet?

JESSA: Asteroid—

SAM: —it's probably nothing, right?

JESSA: I think that light's getting brighter.

DR MOXIE: Danni, are you well?

DANNI: I'll manage boss.

DR MOXIE: Jessa, how's the coffee?

JESSA: Ready for that fresh pot whenever you want. *(Suddenly)* Ugh!

(Startling everyone)

JESSA: Where is Erica? This was supposed to be *her* shift! I'm tired my feet hurt and I want to go home!

SAM: It's definitely nothing. That comet, asteroid, whatever—is definitely nothing and we're all just panicking because it's late, you're all exhausted, I just, I need—

JESSA: —a cigarette?

SAM: —yeah.

JESSA: I wish you'd stop. It's not good for Mae.

SAM: Kid's not even born yet Jessa.

JESSA: That's not the point—

SAM: When Mae gets here we can talk.

JESSA: —god Sam just take care of yourself. It's like you don't actually give a damn about—

SAM: —I give a lot of damns, okay Jessa?

JESSA: —you *don't*. You're going to smoke yourself to death.

SAM: I'm not doing this again—

JESSA: It's not always your choice—someone has to care about you even if it's just a little bit and ugh you—you make me feel, god I just feel like I have, like I have two, two— *(She catches herself.)*

SAM: —*two what* Jessa?

JESSA: —husbands. *(Beat)* to take care of and don't you think one is enough?

SAM: Yeah. Yeah one is all you really need. That's great Jess just fine fantastic I'm going outside. *(She exits to smoke.)*

JESSA: I don't understand how that always happens—

DANNI: Do you fight with Johnny a lot?

JESSA: Not like this. I, we, Johnny—well—

DANNI: Johnny?

JESSA: We actually, we had a fight a few days ago. I don't really understand what's going on with us, and I think I'm bringing it to work and I don't mean to—I know I'm just pissing Sam off, she's annoyed, I'm nagging her so much—

DANNI: It's more complicated than that— *(Beat)* probably—or something—

JESSA: —it's just that we've, me and Johnny, we've been a little, rocky lately. Which is just stupid because he's always been so good, so peaceful and he made me feel—safe you know?

DANNI: Uh-huh.

JESSA: But I don't feel safe right now.

DANNI: Because of the Asteroid?

JESSA: Because of the future—

DANNI: That's what I meant—

JESSA: —because he's leaving me Danni.

DANNI: —*what?*

JESSA: Yeah.

DANNI: You're kidding. He's just gonna walk out on you and the baby?

JESSA: He's not happy. He feels trapped. He's only ever been a trucker and now he wants something more. He wants to go to California and see the sequoias.

DANNI: The sequoias?

JESSA: Largest trees in the world.

DANNI: Well Jesus Christ Jess tell him no he's got to stay here and be a freakin father and forget about the flippin trees—

JESSA: We've talked about it, we've talked a lot and it's just, he feels like he can't raise a kid right now he needs adventure and he needs to become a better person—

DANNI: —well maybe raising a baby will make him a better—

JESSA: —Danni—please. I know okay I know we've talked about it and at first he said it he said he'd stay but all he does now, it's like he's not even a person just a lump he may as well go I can do this on my own. I won't be the first.

DANNI: That's messed up. Does Sam know?

JESSA: No. No and don't tell her yet. Please. She's going to absolutely lose her shit. I can't handle that right now, I'll tell her after he leaves, and then I don't have to worry about getting between them when she tries to kill him.

DANNI: Jeez Jess I'm so sorry.

JESSA: Me too. Kind of, I'm kind of, I don't know how I feel yet. It's like when we were first together I really loved him. I think. No, no I did. But it's been, lately, just—I'm gonna be okay. And soon I'm gonna have Mae and we'll be okay together.

DANNI: Yeah. Yeah. See this is why I don't bother with men—

JESSA: It's not like that. Anyway you and Doc might as well be married so don't read me the riot act alright—

DR MOXIE: What's that?

DANNI: Nothing absolutely nothing boss thanks for checking in.

DR MOXIE: I'm eccentric Jessa I'm not deaf.

JESSA: It's a healthy marriage. Sort of. I would say.

DR MOXIE: Danni is the very best spouse I could have hoped for.

DANNI: Ugh feelings boss don't, don't do this.

DR MOXIE: Our mutually occurring fascination with one another is nothing to be ashamed of my dear.

DANNI: *(To* JESSA*)* This time of night is bizarre you know. Boss is lost in stimulants. He gets all, you know—feelings. *(To* DR MOXIE*)* Easy on the coffee boss. What about your heart?

DR MOXIE: My heart will be fine, Danni. Lightning rarely strikes twice, as you know. *(Beat)* Though I thank you for your concern.

DANNI: It's a loving concern. Also selfish cause if something happens to you we're all totally screwed right?

DR MOXIE: I have faith that your intellectual capacity will carry you far Danni, provided you allow yourself to consider all the variables—

DANNI: Doc—

DR MOXIE: —and don't get lost in your insecurities.

DANNI: I know I know—

(The door opens and SAM *enters.)*

SAM: Jessa I'm sorry—

JESSA: *(Rising)* —I'm sorry Sam, I'm real sorry I should, I don't know leave you alone about it I guess.

(They waver for a moment.)

DR MOXIE: Danni, time?

DANNI: *(She checks her watch and then freaks out a bit.)* Eleven fifty eight woah guys woah we have to um we have to, I need to make sure I've got, um boss are the calculations all set? and do we need anything else from the, um from the car or outside or here or anything?

DR MOXIE: Danni—

DANNI: —nothing is so aggravating as calmness boss—

DR MOXIE: Oscar Wilde well remembered. Danni. Sit.

(DANNI *sits.*)

DANNI: It's just, it's just that this is it—

DR MOXIE: Jessa, I think I'd like a fresh cup of coffee—
do you mind?

JESSA: No, no I don't mind although I don't think
anyone in this diner needs another damn cup of
coffee—

SAM: (*Approaching* DR MOXIE, *she places a hand on his
shoulder*) Doc—

DR MOXIE: All set Sam. Just a few more seconds—

JESSA: —it's like daylight outside I can't even see the
stars—

DANNI: Give it a minute—

JESSA: —I mean if it's going to impact, didn't you say,
you said midnight, didn't you—

DANNI: Boss has it under control, just—

DR MOXIE: Coffee Jessa—

SAM: This is it huh—

JESSA: Oh! (*With a hand over her stomach*) Mae kicked!

SAM: —goose bumps. Now I've got them.

JESSA: I think baby Mae can feel it. Something weird—

DR MOXIE: Jessa—

JESSA: Comin' right up doc—

(JESSA *makes her way to the coffee pot. As she turns it on,
there is a loud noise as the asteroid makes its impact with
the Earth and light comes pouring through the windows.
A beat and then darkness and in the darkness stars start*

*shooting past, first one, then another, until there are
hundreds—thousands—of stars flying through the air
beyond the windows like a computer sequence. Everything
inside the diner is dark except for the stars, which hang from
the ceiling, which shine as they catch the light from the stars
outside.)*

*(JESSA is screaming, clinging to the counter, DANNI is in
her glory, spinning along with the light and the diner, a
huge smile on her face, DR MOXIE observes. SAM initially
tries to comfort JESSA, but soon becomes motion sick, and
wobbles to a corner to retch.)*

DANNI: *(Laughing like crazy)* This is incredible!

DR MOXIE: It's physics.

JESSA: What's happening what's happening what's
going on did it hit us—

DANNI: It hit but not us not us anymore.

(SAM is vomiting.)

JESSA: What is this?!

DANNI: THIS IS TIME TRAVEL!

DR MOXIE: Which should take a few moments. I regret
not offering you some Dramamine, Sam.

SAM: Not—your fault—doc— *(She's having trouble
standing.)*

JESSA: Oh my god oh my god oh my god—HOW?

DANNI: The coffee pot!

JESSA: The coffee pot?

DANNI: The coffee pot is a time machine!

DR MOXIE: Don't give away all our secrets Danni.

DANNI: If it's gonna be just us now Doc we'd better
stop having secrets, oh oh wow look at that, look now
that was a comet! Did you see the tail?

JESSA: All these stars *(Still holding onto the counter she looks around, out the windows)* it's beautiful—

DR MOXIE: Just a few more moments, hang in there Sam—

(A low moan from SAM.)

JESSA: *(Moving away from the counter)* Wow. Just, wow look at this—

DANNI: *(Taking her hand)* it's everything, everything that ever happened that helped to make us—

JESSA: —the womb of the universe—

DR MOXIE: The universe *is* a womb. And three...two... one—

(With a woosh of air the diner comes to a stop, the stars slow down and place themselves back in the sky which is now dark, unobstructed by the glow of the asteroid which remains in the future. Through the windows are giant trees. Cypress and a few sequoia. Somewhere in the distance there is the roar of a large reptile.)

(Inside the Starlight the stars flicker back on.)

(Over the Starlight Diner the moon hangs low and full and yellow.)

(Inside the diner SAM collects herself, wiping her mouth.)

SAM: Ugh.

DANNI: *(Noticing the stars)* Do we have power?

JESSA: Back up generator.

(SAM vomits one last time.)

DR MOXIE: *(Rising, leaving his papers behind him finally, he digs through his bag, searching and then pulling out a large bag of black licorice.)* Eureka!

SAM: My head—

DR MOXIE: *(Offering her the licorice)* Here, have some of these—

SAM: —I hate black licorice— *(But she accepts it grudgingly)* ugh.

(SAM looks up to see DANNI and JESSA together at the window)

SAM: Jessa?

JESSA: *(With a hand on her stomach)* We're okay Sam—

DANNI: *(Realizing she is holding JESSA's hand, drops it, looks awkward)* Sam—sam sorry we didn't warn you about um, the risk of motion sickness—

SAM: You really could have—

JESSA: —you could have warned us about the risk of *motion!*

DR MOXIE: Would you have believed us?

JESSA & SAM: No not at all—

DANNI: Party foul. *(Weak laughter, and then she collects herself)* um, hey yeah super sorry about the secrecy. We weren't even going to bring you but—

DR MOXIE: *(Interrupting)* We would never have journeyed without you. You are integral to the Starlight.

DANNI: Yeah but Jes—

SAM: Danni shut it—

JESSA: But Jes what?

DANNI: *(Finally getting it)* But JES um, we said to ourselves, but *JES* is like the most important person and we should totally take her with us on our journey to the past because who else would make us coffee *(Trailing off)* or something *less* offensive, Danni you nitwit—

JESSA: The *past*? What's going on doc where are we?

(In the distance another roar. It begins to rain softly.)

DR MOXIE: By my best approximation somewhere around sixty-five million years in the past—

DANNI: *(Excitedly)* Which means late Cretaceous. VERY late Cretaceous. Which means, we may be at risk for another asteroid, but—

DR MOXIE: —but not within our lifespan—

DANNI: —which is why—oh, which, never mind—

JESSA: Our lifespan, *our lifespan*? but wait, the past? The Crustacean—

DR MOXIE: —Cretaceous—

JESSA: —what does that mean, exactly, what—wait—

(JESSA has been looking out the windows, shaking her head in disbelief, taking it all in, suddenly overwhelmed, she goes outdoors before anyone can stop her. The door shuts behind her, there is another roar, JESSA screams and comes back in slamming the door behind her)

JESSA: DANNI! Outside—it's so tall, taller than me, there's a, um, I don't even know, feathers and a beak—not a bird—

DANNI: OOH! A beak? Feathers? Did it have four toes?

JESSA: I DIDN'T COUNT THEM!

DANNI: Doesn't matter! It was probably a Nothronychus. *(She's beaming and pulls a pad of paper out of her back pocket.)* That's the first one—

SAM: Hey Ash, can you catch them later, I think we've got a bigger problem on our hands—

(JESSA is clutching the counter, breathing hard, nostrils flared, eyes wide.)

JESSA: Sam—

SAM: *(By her side)* Hey, hey I'm here it's okay.

JESSA: Is there, if this is time travel—can we go forward, can we just go back—

DANNI: She's not taking this so well Sam—

SAM: No shit—

DANNI: I *told* you—

SAM: Danni cork it please—

DR MOXIE: Jessa, I'm afraid there is no forward. Our journey was propelled by the impact of our era's asteroid. We would need to replicate a force of that magnitude in order to journey further in any direction.

SAM: So we're stuck here—

DANNI: So we *get* to *stay* here.

JESSA: Forever?

DR MOXIE: Ad infinitum.

SAM: Forever—forever—wait—I thought, I thought this was just for a little while, until everything, you know, like blew over or we figured out a way to I don't know, destroy the asteroid—

JESSA: Wait—

DR MOXIE: As I've stated—

SAM: —yeah, great force, I know—

JESSA: Wait—

DANNI: Don't worry guys it's gonna be totally awesome okay, like the Starlight is perfect for right now we can sleep in the seats and like eat what's in the kitchen until we learn to hunt and take care of ourselves, this is, this is the closest anyone has ever gotten to experiencing exactly what life was like/ during prehistoric times—

JESSA: /—hold on, hold on, SHUT UP.

DANNI: Hey, Jessa. I know it's scary but—

JESSA: *(To* SAM*)* Did you know?

DANNI: oh shit did I just blow it—

JESSA: You knew.

SAM: Jessa, it's complicated—

JESSA: Complicated—

SAM: —listen, they were going to leave you—

DANNI: Hey, Sam, Jessa, we had reasonable doubts—

DR MOXIE: Giving birth under our present circumstances being a forerunner—

JESSA: —but you, you knew, and you could've told me, and you pretended the comet wasn't a big deal and you acted like, like nothing was going on just the same—

SAM: —and you acted like I had no clue about Johnny so where does that leave us?

DANNI: Oh this is uncomfortable—

JESSA: *(To* DANNI *and* DR MOXIE*)*Get out.

DR MOXIE: Perhaps it's time to gather some specimens.

DANNI: I'd say prime time let's go—

*(*DANNI *grabs some mason jars and exits,* DR MOXIE *right behind her. As they exit, the world of the Cretaceous unfolds around them. They begin collecting specimens.)*

(In the diner SAM *is cleaning.)*

JESSA: Where are we?

SAM: What do you mean, Jessa?

DANNI: Boss, boss I can't believe we made it I can't believe we're finally here would you have believed, like, a year ago a month ago last week!? That this was possible that we could get here?

DR MOXIE: Easy now Danni you don't want to scare off any specimens.

DANNI: No no of course not—it's just it's like Christmas! like straight a's! A grand slam tie-breaker in the thirteenth inning! a total lunar eclipse! and I can't, like, make myself calm down because—well—because—

DR MOXIE: Because?

DANNI: —because it's so beautiful.

JESSA: Where are we, this can't be real, we can't time travel and there can't be dinosaurs and I don't accept that you planned all of this and— *(Realization)* Erica—

SAM: *(Looks sheepish)* uh

JESSA: What did you tell her?

DR MOXIE: It's very beautiful Danni. Look at the sky. All of those stars. Some of them still so young, and brighter than we've ever seen them. The air quality is much better, the foliage larger and—

DANNI: —and?

DR MOXIE: —and you *look* happy, Danni, you look more awake. You look—like you're finally getting enough oxygen.

JESSA: *What did you tell her?*

SAM: I just, I said you guys needed some extra funds and, I mean, I had some tickets for a Dead concert and she owed me a favor anyway—

JESSA: —extra funds?

SAM: Well it's not a lie—

JESSA: And now you're concerned with my finances?

SAM: Well you've got a kid coming and your husband's leaving you so I thought, gee what a prime time to try and help a friend in need—

JESSA: Help me? Help me Sam you *live in your truck*—

SAM: By choice.

DANNI: Boss cut it out you're gonna make me blush or something.

DR MOXIE: The late cretaceous suits you Danni. I don't know if I could say that for many.

DANNI: Well it's a swell place. I mean it's like everything I ever wanted and the only thing that could make it better would be like—

DR MOXIE: The um, the Diamondbacks?

JESSA: You think you can do better? You think I need to be looked after, I can't take care of myself?

SAM: Well—

JESSA: —Jesus Christ Sam—

SAM: What were you gonna do jess? No husband? On your diner salary and tips and I don't know luck?

JESSA: Well it doesn't matter anymore does it because apparently we are trapped in the past and oh my god—

SAM: jess—

JESSA: —I—I'm going to have a baby here. I have to raise Mae, *here.*

SAM: We've got a doctor.

DANNI: Nah boss not baseball. *(Beat)* my folks.

JESSA: *(She runs to the coffee pot turning it on and off but with no luck.)* Isn't, isn't this thing supposed to be a time machine? How *(On)* do you *(Off)* get it *(On)* to work? *(Off on off)* auuugh! *(Turning on SAM)* You—you—I— *(She loses steam.)* I can't believe—how—

SAM: Jess—it's going to be okay. it's gonna have to be okay. Because we couldn't stay there, you know, and what kind of life did we have there anyway? even before the asteroid.

JESSA: I had a dog—

SAM: I'm sorry.

JESSA: Johnny's dead?

DANNI: It's weird to think about it, about the fact that they're probably, well—dead—

SAM: I mean, I don't know if it counts—are they dead if, I mean, we didn't go forward—and, and I guess that means they're stuck—in the future so yeah, probably, they're—

DR MOXIE: While I am reluctant to entertain notions of fantasy, in this instance it might be easier to envision time as linear—

DANNI: —oh, no boss, you don't have to—

DR MOXIE: —just this once—

JESSA: I have to sit down.

(SAM *helps* JESSA *to a chair:*)

SAM: Maybe I should've told you Jess but I didn't think you'd come if, if you knew—

JESSA: and my parents.

DR MOXIE: —for if time were linear, than perhaps it could be theorized that rather than already deceased your parents are still *(Beat)* yet to come.

DANNI: *(Beat)* That helps, actually. It does. And maybe, I don't know. I mean I'm like still a product of the two of them. Whether they like it or not and I can take the information they've given me and put it to real good use here.

DR MOXIE: Indeed. You're going to lose that wasp—

DANNI: AH! *(She lunges to catch it.)*

SAM: —Danni and the doc, they didn't want to risk it but I—

JESSA: i'm all alone—

SAM: —I couldn't leave you, Jessa. I couldn't just, let you die—

JESSA: *(Beat)* and how do you know I'll live?

SAM: This, this is the best choice we've got—

DANNI: Got it!

DR MOXIE: Well done.

DANNI: Boss—

DR MOXIE: Danni—

DANNI: I'm glad you're here. Or whatever—I'm glad you're—I don't know around and that you've been around when, it's hard. When it was hard—

DR MOXIE: —I'm proud of you Danni. I'm very proud of who you have become. You're going to be a fine scientist.

DANNI: Thank you.

DR MOXIE: *(He grabs his left arm.)* oh—

DANNI: What's wrong boss? Are you okay?

DR MOXIE: *(He recovers.)* Yes. Yes I believe so. Just a sudden passing pain. My body, perhaps, throwing off the remaining strain of travelling through so many eras—

DANNI: Yeah?

DR MOXIE: Yes. Yes I think so. *(He gives* DANNI *a pat)* Don't worry.

DANNI: I—okay.

JESSA: You should have asked me Sam. You should have told me everything you knew and asked me—

SAM: I—

JESSA: If you had asked me— (*She gets up, walks towards the door*)

SAM: (*Running after her*) Jess, you can't—

(SAM *grabs her arm and* JESSA *pulls away*)

JESSA: —don't touch me!

SAM: I'm sorry, I'm so sorry—

JESSA: —I would have said yes. (*She exits.*)

SAM: SHIT (*She hits *something* with her fist*)

(*Silence*)

(*The door opens again,* SAM *looks up hopefully but it's not* JESSA *it's* DANNI *looking thrilled as she juggles several mason jars full of specimens—plants, pinecones, bugs, etc.* DR MOXIE *strolls in behind her, his hands covered in something prehistorically foul.*)

DR MOXIE: FIELD WORK!

DANNI: Sam. SAM SAM SAM. You HAVE to see what we got, I mean, we didn't even go twenty feet—

SAM: It's not a good time guys.

DANNI: (*Lining jars on the counter*) pinecones, mud, and *look* at this wasp—ugh, nasty. And Sam! You'll never even believe it, there's a whole ocean out there!

SAM: That's really cool.

DR MOXIE: (*Of whatever is on his hands*) I'm going to attempt to salvage enough of this for an adequate sample— (*He exits to the kitchen.*)

DANNI: (*Looking around*) Where's Jessa?

SAM: She, she left.

DANNI: Left? Shit—outside? Alone?

SAM: She left she might not come back it's my fault—I—

DANNI: No Sam you're good, she—

SAM: I thought I was doing the right thing—

DANNI: You did the right thing. What were you gonna do leave her to die?

SAM: I mean, she's right. Didn't we do that to everyone else?

DANNI: It's different—

SAM: *(Upset)* It's not *different* Danni! It's the same, it's, I mean, I don't know I guess—I don't really have anyone except—

DANNI: —except?

SAM: —never mind.

DANNI: *(Beat)* listen Sam. If this is real, if this is it now, if this is our new world—I'm not gonna lie. I'm scared. Ok? I'm piss my pants terrified actually because who knows if it's going to work, if we can actually live out here and I mean, fuck everyone's seen Jurassic Park so it's not like I'm unawares as to how low on the food chain we are. and all of this really cool research we can do? Literally no way to share it with anyone. *(Beat)* So I get it. I have parents, Sam. Kind of frustrating parents but they're still good people. And I had dreams—

SAM: This doesn't have to be it—Danni maybe we can figure out a way back?

DANNI: No uh uh no way didn't you hear the boss? We don't have a way back. Coffee pot only goes one way.

SAM: Different dreams then, huh?

DANNI: Yeah. Yeah I got new dreams now. Dreams for here. I wanna build my own wunderkammer. You know what that is?

SAM: No Danni I don't know what that is.

DANNI: A cabinet of wonders. I'm going to collect as many amazing things as I can find. And then I'm going to build the most amazing tree house lab, and I'm going to line everything up, and log it— *(She pulls out her notebook)* in this. It's going to be the most amazing scientific journal nobody will ever get to see.

SAM: Aren't you and the doc worried about I don't know—tainting the past or something?

DANNI: I mean. probably.

SAM: Oh. Okay.

DANNI: I mean who cares right? Time is a loop so whatever we did back here we already did before the time we lived in. It's not like our journey back here started when we came back in time. We already messed up whatever we were going to mess up. Shit. Maybe we even caused the asteroid or whatever but who knows.

SAM: Danni you're giving me a headache.

DANNI: Whatever old man. *(Beat)* Listen, Sam, don't you think you should look for Jessa—

SAM: —she's really angry with me.

DANNI: I know. But maybe—don't give up?

SAM: She'll come back. She needs time to cool down. Accept all of this.

DANNI: Yeah. Yeah. *(Beat)* she probably won't get eaten.

SAM: Very helpful Danni.

DANNI: It's really too bad about that asteroid huh?

SAM: *(Stares at DANNI)* Yeah.

DANNI: I mean, I was like so close to graduating. Well. No. No I wasn't but like, I was on my way. And boss, he just figured out how to mess with all this space-time stuff. He could have gotten rich.

SAM: At least he—you both—saved some lives.

DANNI: Yeah. And don't worry he's not all about repopulating or anything.

SAM: No because that would be crazy.

DANNI: It really would. In this era. I mean.

SAM: Thank goodness for common sense. *(Beat)* Your wunderkammer sounds real cool.

DANNI: Thanks. My dad has one. *(Beat)* Had one. Or, will have. I'm not really sure.

SAM: Yeah?

DANNI: Yeah. I'm going to miss him. My mom was, god, she hated the way—I mean when it comes down to it I think she hated, like, you know who I really am because she loved me, I know she loved me—but it was this really idealized version of what she thought I should be—

SAM: Parents.

DANNI: I'll miss them. My dad. My mom too.

SAM: I'm gonna miss my truck.

DANNI: What if this is a horrible mistake. *(Beat)* What if the boss and I, we think we're doing good but like. I mean it's just the four of us now. Forever. And soon we'll have Jessa's kid and I'm, like, so—so—lonely—so—um um sam—

(DANNI leans in, kisses SAM and for a minute it's kind of the best thing in the universe but SAM's got her eyes open so it's obvious how it's going to end.)

(They pull apart.)

SAM: Danni, listen—

DANNI: No, Sam, no, it's cool I get it—you don't have to say anything okay. It. I just—

SAM: I know. *(She gives* DANNI *a hug, long embrace, holds her real tight.)* It's done.

DANNI: It's done.

(A moment of silence. DANNI *and* SAM *remain hugging.)*

SAM: It's not you—

*(*DANNI, *laughing, wiping away tears,* DANNI *and* SAM *pull apart:)*

DANNI: Dude I know—

SAM: What do you mean—

DANNI: It's Jessa—

SAM: *(Panicked)* Danni shut up—how do you—

DANNI: It's not a secret—wait. Is it a secret? *(Beat)* Everyone knows you're like head over heels—

SAM: —shut up! *(Beat)* How?

DANNI: But you two, you two are like Nora and the Doctor—

SAM: *(Beat)* Who?

DANNI: Ibsen?

SAM: *(Beat)* What?

DANNI: She knows you love her, okay? This is not news.

SAM: You don't know what you're talking about, Danni— *(A pained look)* you can't say anything, don't *say anything*—

DANNI: *(Beat)* Sam—I think, I think she loves you too—

SAM: Danni—I mean she's married—still, she's still married. To a man—

DANNI: —I don't think that matters. I don't think that matters one bit I think she loves you and given our current circumstances I think that's what matters the most, I think—I think that you should— *(Beat) shit* Sam. I think you should tell her—

SAM: Oh god. Oh god I can't— She, what if she, you know I'm like, I'm not—I'm *(She gestures to herself.)* Look at me—I'm—

DANNI: Perfect? *(Beat)* It just comes down to what's on the inside you know?

SAM: What, like guts and stuff?

DANNI: Well, yeah, guts but like—but like other really beautiful shit too you know?

SAM: Yeah. Yeah. *(A breath)* I do.

DANNI: Wow. revelations in the past. *(Beat)* This is awkward. *(Beat)* I like that the stars in here are still lit. that's um pretty magical huh?

SAM: Yeah. Yeah the Starlight is well, pretty magical. *(Laughing)* we're cool Danni right?

DANNI: I think so.

SAM: Is the doc gonna be alright? He kind of vanished.

DANNI: He stuck his hands in some ancient pine sap, he's probably gonna be busy for a few hours—

(A clap of thunder. The rain falls harder.)

SAM: *(Looking out the window)* It's pouring out there.

(In the distance JESSA screams.)

DANNI: Shit—

(DANNI and SAM rise and run out the door, exiting the diner.)

(A flash of lightning illuminates the world outside the windows, outlining the trees as they're blown by the

wind and in the distance highlighting the form of a large dinosaur.)

(DR MOXIE enters the diner from the kitchen, wiping his hands with a dishtowel. He's humming, looking down. Oblivious to the world around him.)

DR MOXIE: Vastness is not a concept unique to the universe. Are we not all born from stars? What you hold within has held everything that has ever been. Love is a simple truth. Life and death and time and motion, they're all a lie but love—love— *(He looks up.)* Oh. No-one here. Well.

(DR MOXIE examines the jars and their specimens, taking time to pick each one up, hold it up to the stars inside the diner, he makes noises of approval, he stops to examine one of the last containers most closely. Inside is Urosaurus Ornatus, DANNI's lizard. DR MOXIE makes a low noise of disapproval. He removes the lid, he removes the lizard.)

DR MOXIE: Urosaurus Ornatus. *(Beat)* Outside, Danni.

(DR MOXIE wraps it in the dishtowel. He holds it. He places it on the floor, lifts his foot. After a few excruciating beats, he stoops to pick it back up, placing it in the jar once more.)

(DR MOXIE exits to the kitchen, returning almost instantly with a slice of pie. He sits next to Urosaurus Ornatus. He removes the lid once more and the two share the pie.)

(DR MOXIE and Urosaurus Ornatus sit together in silence finishing the pie. With his last bite, DR MOXIE rises to bring the plate to the kitchen, but as he rises, he falls back into the seat. He moans, and grabs chest, coughing.)

(The stars in the diner begin to flicker out one by one.)

(After a few moments, when almost all the stars are dark, the door to the diner is thrown open. DANNI and SAM enter, supporting JESSA who is limping. All three women are soaking wet and streaked with mud.)

(DR MOXIE *does not move.*)

SAM: Doc! We need some help—

DANNI: She hurt her ankle boss—

SAM: —is the power out? How long has it been dark?

DANNI: —here jess here sit I'll see if we have ice— *(She exits to the kitchen)*

JESSA: I'm alright I'm okay I just slipped—

SAM: —why? Why did you go out there on your own you have no idea what's out there you could have gotten killed—

JESSA: Sam, sam it's okay, I'm just, just a little soaked and muddy and my ankle is sore but I can move it—

SAM: *(Kneeling in front of her)* It's swollen, it's swollen and what about Mae, when you fell, did you land on her? Is that how pregnancy works? I don't even—did you hurt anything else are you scratched are you bleeding?

(SAM *is searching* JESSA *all over for signs of injury,* JESSA *reaches down to take her hands,* SAM *suddenly aware of their contact, freezes.)*

JESSA: Sam. Sam. Look at me. I'm safe. I'm here.

SAM: jessa when you left, when you ran out there i should have followed you i don't know why i let you go alone—

JESSA: I didn't give you much choice—

(DANNI *runs back in from the kitchen holding a bag of frozen peas.)*

DANNI: Here here it's the best I could find—

JESSA: *(Taking the peas)* this is good this is perfect. *(She places the bag on her ankle.)* it's really okay. I'm fine.

(SAM *and* DANNI *stare at* JESSA *for a minute, and then exhale together. Together the women notice that all the stars but one have gone dark.)*

DANNI: So that's it for the stars huh?

SAM: Generator's out? That was fast, but for what Tommy paid for it I'm not surprised.

JESSA: No, it's hanging on, look—there's still one star, one star is still lit.

SAM: But the stars outside, they're so much brighter than I've ever seen them—

JESSA: And the moon—

SAM: —So big, so yellow, so low—

JESSA: —what were those birds?

DANNI: Not birds. Pterosaurs.

SAM: Too big.

JESSA: *(Agreeing)* Too big.

DANNI: *(She has noticed* DR MOXIE'*s stillness.)* Hey boss—

SAM: *(To* JESSA*)* you're all right?

(DANNI *approaches* DR MOXIE. *She sees the lizard, takes the jar, places a hand on* DR MOXIE'*s.)*

JESSA: I'm all right.

DANNI: Hey guys—guys—

(DANNI *moves her hand from* DR MOXIE'*s hand, to his shoulder, to his face. His head is bowed his body slouched.)*

SAM: *(Crossing to* DANNI*)* Is he—

DANNI: —boss—boss—

JESSA: *(Hands over her mouth)* no—

DANNI: BOSS—

SAM: *(She takes* DR MOXIE'*s wrist to feel for a pulse, after a few moments she lets it drop)* Danni—

DANNI: How? HOW?

(The three women stand in the diner together in the darkness.)

(The rain grows softer.)

DANNI: I wasn't here. I wasn't here with him and now what, now I'm just alone?

SAM: None of us are alone. None of us are alone here okay?

JESSA: There's a blanket, in the office, I can't *(She tries to get up but can't walk.)* Danni?

DANNI: Yeah. Yeah I'll get it— *(She exits, and comes back with a small blanket, placing it over* DR MOXIE*)* Boss. *(She sits next to him, still holding on to the lizard.)* I'm sorry. I shouldn't have—I know you said not to bring him but—he was, the colors, I really love blue. And I've never. I've never had a pet before so I thought—

SAM: —we should bury him—

JESSA: In the morning.

DANNI: I wanted you to live in the tree house. With me, my wunderkammer, that was, it was supposed to be for both of us. *(Beat, she looks over at* JESSA *and* SAM*)* he was like, well, he was family.

SAM: *(Nods)* We're all family.

JESSA: Better than family.

DANNI: This is it.

SAM: I can't wait to see what this place looks like when the sun rises—

DANNI: I mean. We're all going to die here—

JESSA: Danni—

SAM: *(She rests her hand on* JESSA's *shoulder.)* let her.

DANNI: —we're going to die out here and is that really better than before is that so much better than dying with everyone else we're lost in time out here. *(Beat)* it was so cool. It seemed so cool when we figured out we could do it when we realized, that we could come here and take you and take the diner and skip out on death but shit *(Laughs weakly)* we didn't—boss. I mean I don't even know if this is real maybe it's all just a crazy dream or a hallucination or maybe we're all just already dead—

SAM: Danni—

JESSA: Mae's kicking. I think, when I fell, I think she got scared and now she's tossing and turning— *(She has her hand over her stomach)*

DANNI: May I? *(She approaches* JESSA *and places a hand on her baby bump,* SAM *does the same)*

SAM: That's really something.

JESSA: I know.

DANNI: I'm gonna, I've got to—I think I might— *(She heads to the door.)* I—

SAM: *(Nods)* go. We'll stay with him.

DANNI: I'll be back before sunrise.

SAM: Okay.

JESSA: Be careful—

*(*DANNI *exits.)*

SAM: Jess—

JESSA: I'm here. I'm okay.

SAM: Me too. Me too. Forever, okay? As long as forever is here—

JESSA: I know. I know.

SAM: Moxie's gone.

JESSA: What was it, how—

SAM: God. I don't know. Maybe his heart—

JESSA: He may as well have stayed—

SAM: Don't say that. He got us here.

JESSA: Yeah. Yeah. *(Beat)* What do you think it was like? I mean, when the asteroid hit—what do you think happened to—to everyone?

SAM: I don't know. I've been trying not to think about it.

JESSA: Me too. *(Beat)* But, but I can't stop. I can't stop thinking about how they died. Everyone we used to know, if they if they were burned or if they didn't get hit right away, or if they drowned—

SAM: Drowned?

JESSA: If the asteroid hit the ocean—

SAM: Oh. Oh god.

JESSA: Like, I keep thinking—I have a cousin who lives in New York City. What if the asteroid hit the ocean, and it flooded New York? What if he was on the subway, and the subway flooded and everyone in the tunnels just, they couldn't breathe, or leave, or—

SAM: That's awful that's awful—

JESSA: —I know but I can't stop thinking about it when I close my eyes I just see water and light and I can hear someone screaming, like when I was out there and I couldn't see anything because it was so dark and then I was falling and I heard someone screaming and after, when I landed when my body stopped moving, after, I realized that it was me. Who was screaming it was me. *(Beat)* and now I'm worried that maybe I'm screaming all of the time only I don't know it's me and maybe I'll never stop.

SAM: Jess—jess you're not screaming.

JESSA: What if I am but you can't hear me because you're screaming too? And you'll just never know? Sam—Sam I can't do this. I'm terrified. I'm so scared. Everyone is gone, and I'm gonna have a baby and I just feel so alone Sam— *(She reaches out, grasping for something to hold onto—she finds SAM's hand.)* Sam. Don't let go—

SAM: I won't. Jess. I won't. Ever.

(The diner is quiet for a while. The star that is still lit is shining brightly.)

(SAM inhales. Exhales.)

SAM: Jess, I—I need to say something. I, should have said this, I should have—a long time ago, okay

JESSA: Yeah, yeah okay—

SAM: Jess—jessa i—when I look at you it—it's like everything I ever felt for the Starlight only more? Only cause your eyes are galaxies and your heartbeat, god it's like I can hear it no matter where I am and it's just this sort of slow steady beating in the background of my universe and jess I know I'm not, I'm not *like* Johnny and I never will be but maybe, maybe I can be better because I would never leave you and every time, every night when *you* left and I had to watch you *go* it was—my heart hurt so much. And I think you and Mae and everything you are together, mother and daughter, i want—i want to help you raise her. i, you might not think I'm good enough or just *enough* but— but I am.

JESSA: Sam. *(She reaches out.)* come here.

(SAM does.)

JESSA: Your heart hurt? *(She reaches out to touch* SAM *in the center of her chest. Over her heart)* here?

SAM: So—so much—it's just. I need you to know—

JESSA: —you're just. You're so—

SAM: —different?

JESSA: Beautiful.

SAM: *(She takes* JESSA's *hand in hers, brings it to her mouth, kisses it,)* Jessa. I'm scared too. But Jess, Jessa—I love—

*(*JESSA *pulls* SAM *in and kisses her and* SAM *responds eagerly. They are lost in one another and there are shooting stars flying past the windows of the Starlight. For a moment, it is just the two of them, and then* JESSA *pulls away, just slightly—)*

JESSA: I know.

*(*SAM *pulls away a bit.)*

SAM: —I—okay.

JESSA: And—

SAM: *(Eagerly)* and?

JESSA: —and *fuck* the sequoias!

SAM: Fuck the sequoias! *(Laughter)*

JESSA: *(Beat)* And I love you too. *(Beat)* you know your eyes are the same brown as Johnny's and your hair—I wouldn't be at all surprised if Mae looks just like *you.*

SAM: Just like *me?*

JESSA: *Just* like you.

SAM: Well. *(With a hand on* JESSA's *belly)* Well. Welcome to the world then, little baby Mae. Welcome to the world.

(A dinosaur shrieks in the distance.)

(A bang as the door to the diner is flung open and DANNI *runs back in.)*

DANNI: Hey! WOW. Okay cool. Good. Good that's great actually I'm so happy for you guys but—

SAM: —but?

DANNI: Um, um up in the sky?

JESSA: Yeah?

DANNI: We miscalculated. The other asteroid? It's on its way.

JESSA: *(Taking* SAM's *hand)* what do you mean?

DANNI: It's going to hit us. *(Beat)* but listen. That asteroid? I can, it can help us— *(She strides to the coffee pot.)* I think I can get us out of here.

SAM: *(getting it)* A force of great magnitude—and then, what? Like, back? Like back to normal?

DANNI: Well. No. I don't think there is a *normal* anymore. Or, it's different now.

JESSA: We can't fix it?

DANNI: There's nothing to fix. *(Beat)* But we can't stay here. We can't die here like the boss—we can't stay here where science doesn't even exist yet, okay? Where we'll just like be alone until—until we're gone. I can get us I can *take* us *(Beat)* somewhere else.

JESSA: Where?

DANNI: "I don't know yet. I don't know where we're going from here. But I promise. It won't be boring."

SAM: *(Chuckles)* David Bowie. *(Beat)* Alright.

DANNI: Alright?

JESSA: We trust you, Danni.

SAM: Yeah. Tell us what you need.

DANNI: Well. Well *(Playing with the coffee pot)* power. For one thing.

JESSA: We still have some power, look— *(She points to the star that is still lit.)* is it enough? Do you think?

DANNI: I don't know—but I want to try.

SAM: Should we, I mean, when will it hit us? Should we shut the generator down until the asteroid's closer?

DANNI: Yeah. Yes. Yes we should shut it down for now.

JESSA: When will it get here Danni?

DANNI: I don't know. *(She gathers up some of* DR MOXIE's *papers.)* but, I can figure it out.

SAM: I'll go turn off the generator.

JESSA: *(She grabs onto* SAM *tighter.)* Sam—

SAM: I'll come back.

JESSA: —okay— *(She lets go.)*

*(*SAM *exits.)*

*(*DANNI *sits down across from* DR MOXIE *and sorts through the papers.)*

DANNI: It's going to be different.

JESSA: I know.

(Darkness as the last star goes out.)

END OF PLAY

www.ingramcontent.com/pod-product-compliance
Lightning Source LLC
Chambersburg PA
CBHW070030110426
42741CB00035B/2716